CHOOSE

HAPPINESS

Unapologetically

With Resistance and Persistence

Author

JAMIE S. RALLIFORD

ISBN: 979-8-9887883-1-7 (Paperback)

ISBN: 979-8-9887883-0-0 (Ebook)

DEDICATION

This book is dedicated to all women who want to reach their highest potential. This book serves as a guiding light through tough times, and to help you find happiness and possibilities in tough situations. Its pages are packed with wisdom that will help you push through struggles or hardships - so you can live the joyous existence you deserve.

TABLE OF CONTENTS

INTRODUCTION

Are you tired of pretending to be someone you're not? Do you feel like you're not good enough? What if you didn't have to fear? What if you could choose happiness unapologetically?

The world is full of individuals who lack confidence in their worth. Low self-esteem can be an invisible handicap that prevents people from achieving their true potential, leaving them feeling helpless and unable to live the life they deserve. It's a difficult condition; studies show it affects 85% of the population. For some, these feelings can paralyze and prevent them from achieving their full potential, especially if they deal with their self-doubts alone. (Better Health)

Why People Hide And Pretend Versus Get Help

One of the scariest things we can do in this life is let ourselves be seen. To be vulnerable. To risk being judged and found wanting. It's much easier to play it safe, put on a mask and hide who we are, versus reveal our low self-esteem. However, pretending to be okay when you are not can cause more internal harm than good, and vulnerability can unlock your desired freedom. Take it from me. I wore this mask of concealment for a long time until I was forced to reveal the truth.

Side A

Growing up, I was taught to keep my personal matters within the family. I had a seemingly perfect childhood and enjoyed music because it was always an outlet for me. In college, life had other plans for me: an unplanned pregnancy that brought a different kind of music into my life - being controlled with no voice.

I was shocked to find out that I was pregnant and nervous to reveal the news to my mother. My mother had already planned my life. I would go to school, build a career, get married, and then have children. My mom laying out this plan caused me to feel unsure about my life and if I wanted to have a baby. I couldn't cover up my challenge for too long because my belly grew bigger.

Although I wasn't sure, the decision had been made for me. My mother let me know that, based on her religion, my only option was to have a baby if I intended to stay under her roof and continue my home life as I knew it. Therefore, I went with what was expected of me. As a result, I doubted my ability to decide things for myself, which led me down a path of questioning myself and my ability.

Side B

Through self-reflection, training, coaching, and life lessons, I had to forgive myself for not being perfect and give myself the grace to move forward and be happy. I no longer punish myself or beat myself up. I chose to be happy. The challenges that caused me to be ashamed actually helped me build strong resilience and perseverance in pursuit of my purpose.

This book will inspire anyone who suffers from imposter syndrome, self-doubt or an inability to open up, while providing a new outlook on life. Writing this book is my way of sharing my stories about resilience and persistence to uplift you in the face of adversity.

As you will discover from the personal stories in this book, facing your struggles can lead you down paths filled with hope and success! This book will help you find the strength to press onward, even when self-doubt and perceived vulnerabilities try to hold you back.

Choose Happiness Unapologetically with Resilience and Persistence offers an inspiring path to discovering your inner strength, power, and resilience. It helps readers become the most authentic version of themselves: confident, unafraid, and content with life. The chapters are presented uniquely; instead of the traditional layout, they're arranged like music tracks! Dividing into *Side A*, where you will learn how to overcome common obstacles that can stand in your way - from fear and anxiety to low self-esteem. Then flip over to *Side B*, which provides direction on defining what kind of life you want and guides you towards living a fulfilling future, alongside a collection of upbeat songs as chapter titles for inspiration.

If you are ready to choose happiness unapologetically, then I urge you to read this book. I went from self-doubt questioning where I belong, to now knowing I belong in ANY DAMN ROOM that I am in. I am good enough, deserving, hard-working, and don't care what others think. That's the freedom this book will help you to achieve.

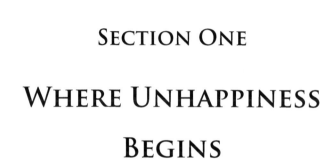

SECTION ONE

WHERE UNHAPPINESS BEGINS

Choose Happiness Unapologetically

TRACK 1

THE MIRACLE CHILD

"You will be in pain for the rest of your life,
and you will never have children."

That's what the doctors told my mother ten years before I was born. I'm sure you figured it out by now, but the doctors were wrong.

Side A

My Life

My name is Jamie S. Davis, and I was born in New York to American parents. My father is from Mobile, Alabama; my mother is from Queens, New York; and my maternal grandparents are from South Carolina. Despite being told she would never be able to conceive by medical professionals due to her endometriosis diagnosis in her twenties, my mother persevered for 10 years before giving birth to me in 1977. Thus, doctors considered me a miracle baby.

I was the only child and only grandchild on my mother's side. I loved being an only child because not only was I spoiled by my parents but also by my grandparents, who loved me deeply. I felt every bit of my family's love.

Growing up, I felt the influence of my hardworking family in every aspect of my life. My grandfather, who had only a fourth-grade education and couldn't read or write, was both a janitor and handyman. My grandmother went from housekeeping to homemaking after surviving breast cancer. My mom wished for more out of life, which drove her success. After she graduated high school, she was employed at The New York Telephone Company along with singing lead vocals in an aspiring R&B group, "The Inverts," until the early 1970s before I was born. Her group opened for Gladys Knight and the Pips at the Apollo in 1967. Her love for performing and music has impacted me tremendously.

I was an only child, but I was never lonely. I grew up surrounded by tons of family. I loved music, riding my bike, and playing double dutch, and handball. I am thankful for my carefree and blissful childhood, a time in which I was able to be exactly that - a child. My mother played an instrumental role, creating structure while simultaneously showing immense love and providing the best of everything she could offer her family. She was an excellent mom to me, and a supportive wife to my father.

Until age five, I lived in the building next to the skating rink in Lefrak City in Queens. Afterward, we rented a house on my mother's childhood block in East Elmhurst, next door to my grandmother and grandfather. I loved growing up in East Elmhurst because many family members were nearby. I have many fond memories.

As my mother dreamed of home ownership, she set her sights on a nearby Co-op. However, this plan was met with resistance from my grandfather. My grandfather disapproved of the co-op because he didn't want me to miss out on the joys of having an outdoor space - he had already built me a sandbox and swing set in his backyard, plus a portable pool! In response to his disapproval, my grandfather made my parents an offer they couldn't refuse he agreed to help cover the down payment costs for a home in Jamaica, Queens - complete with a yard so I could play safely outside like before!

Our new home was innovative yet unique, but I missed living in East Elmhurst, next door to my grandparents, and with family within walking distance. However, my Uncle lived in the basement of our new house, and I was happy I could still see him.

My parents were excited about our new home, and they planned to celebrate by having a housewarming barbecue on July 4th, 1986. It was going to be big with friends and family. I was also excited about the housewarming because I loved it when my family got together; there was always so much love and fun, and I'd see all my cousins. We enjoyed each other and always had a good time together.

My parents planned the housewarming for months. On the morning of July 4th, my mother entered the basement where my Uncle lived. I don't recall what she was going downstairs for, but I remember her calling my Uncle as she proceeded downstairs. My dad was outside in the back preparing the grill and backyard, and I was inside the house being an excited, happy kid that knew she and her cousins were about to have a good day!

My excitement changed when I heard my mother screaming from the basement. She called down to my Uncle on her way downstairs as she always did when she'd go downstairs into the laundry room or when she may have had to enter his apartment. But this time, he didn't answer her, and I guess she thought he was sleeping, so she went inside his apartment and woke him up to help with the B.B.Q. preparation, only to find his body on the bathroom floor. We found out later that my Uncle suffered a heart attack and died from the hardening of the arteries. A condition neither my parents nor grandparents were aware that he suffered from.

The energy and plans for that day were shifted as my parents awaited the coroner after the paramedics left. My other aunt and Uncle came over, picked me up and brought me back to their home to spend time with my cousins while my mom and dad sorted things out at our house. Family and friends still gathered the night of the 4th to support my family in the mourning of my Uncle; it was not the planned fun-filled housewarming. This day was the first of three times in my life that I can recall seeing my mother cry. Because the loss of my

Uncle happened during preparation for an exciting occasion, I still hesitate to get excited about upcoming family events as I always feel like something terrible will happen. However, I'm grateful when we can gather, and things go as planned.

Side B

My mother's life took an unexpected turn after her brother's passing. Two Jehovah's Witnesses knocked on our door, one of whom would become my mom's spiritual mentor guiding her to Scriptures that brought comfort to this sorrowful time. Inevitably their visits increased, and she began intensely studying with them—an endeavor that significantly altered my existence as I knew it. Suddenly birthdays, Christmas, Thanksgiving, and every other holiday we cherished were no longer a part of life.

As an only child going through a religious transformation, every day became something entirely new. Faith-based values surrounded me. From weeknight meetings to Sunday services at the Kingdom Hall and personal Bible studies - my life during this time was immersed in religious teachings. While attending the Kingdom Hall wasn't quite my cup of tea, it instilled important moral principles that would shape me for many years. I appreciate being raised in a Christian home with Christian values instilled in me early on.

Throughout my childhood, there were changes and growth within my family. However, my constant was that I was a miracle child and loved unconditionally by my parents and family. My family's love was the backbone of everything that I did.

TRACK 2

I GOT IT MADE

"When a team takes ownership of its problems, the problem gets solved. It is true on the battlefield, it is true in business, and it is true in life." Jocko Willink

Growing up, I attended public school and tested into the Talented & Gifted program (T.A.G). in Kindergarten. T.A.G. was designed to give children deemed gifted, based on an entrance examination, advanced coursework to keep them ahead of the curve.

I began my T.A.G. journey the beginning of the 1st grade, where I met several peers who have become lifelong friends. I was in classes with the same students from the first to the fifth grades. The natural progression for T.A.G. students graduating from Louis Armstrong Elementary School was to apply and attend Louis Armstrong Middle School (IS 227) upon graduation.

IS 227 was one of the best junior high schools in Queens, N.Y. at the time. The application process was intense and competitive, and the school did not accept many students. Being in T.A.G., we were considered some of the most intelligent kids in public school. Therefore, it was almost a given that we'd get into the prestigious middle school IS 227. That was the case for many of my classmates, but not for me.

Side A

I remember awaiting the IS 227 acceptance letter. Both of my best friends had received theirs and had been accepted. On the other hand, I received a rejection letter stating they were sorry they couldn't take me at this time. I was devastated! I cried non-stop for about 48 hours.

The day after I received the letter, my mother went to the school to meet with the administration to better understand what happened. My mother was planning to head into the office after stopping at the school, so she arrived early. It turns out that I wasn't the only student who hadn't been accepted, and other parents there needed answers.

My mother happened to be the first parent in a line of about 50-60 other parents waiting for the principal's office to open. They allowed my mother and a few others inside the building when they opened the doors. My mother was asked to sign in and wait in the office, as were the few other parents that made it inside.

When the school began calling names, the principal said he would only see my mother and that all the others waiting would have to call and schedule an appointment. Thank God my mom was early and arrived first!

At the school meeting, my mother was stunned to find out that I had been wrongly denied admission into the school. My beloved teacher didn't check the box indicating my talented and gifted status, which resulted in me being denied admission.

Without hesitation, my mother took prompt action: writing letters and submitting an amended application on my behalf. Thankfully this initiative paid off; within two weeks of pursuing it, I gained entry into IS 227 middle school -

something which meant so much to me as a fifth grader that I would have rather gotten a job than attend anywhere else!

Side B

When you want results, procrastination is not the answer. My mother's early arrival at the school and being the only parent seen that day taught me to show up early for the things that matter most. There are things in the world that we can't control, such as a mistake on my teacher's behalf. However, people who show up early have a better chance of getting what they want. Showing up for ourselves and being prepared is a great way to have an advantage whenever there is intense competition such as in my situation.

When I didn't get into the school I hoped for, I wasn't willing to go to another school; I was prepared to drop out of school and get a job. This experience showed me not to give up on plan A and shift to plan B so quickly. Evaluating the results to see why the original plan didn't work is critical to have enough time to fix any errors. Instead of my mother making plans for me to go to another school, she was determined to find out why I didn't get into the school I wanted to go to.

As a result of my mother's hard work, I began my junior high journey at the Louis Armstrong Middle School, IS 227, in the Fall of 1988. Hands down, those junior high school years were some of the most memorable times of my life.

Success

To be successful, which brings true happiness, you must be resilient and persistent in your goals. Success doesn't come without planning. To achieve your goals, it's essential to have a goal-oriented mindset and a results-driven attitude. Starting with writing your goals gives you direction on where to go next – figuring out the steps needed to make that dream happen as quickly as possible before any deadlines approach. Lastly, reflecting upon what worked well or if additional steps need to be taken after seeing initial results make up the process for true success.

TRACK 3

JOY & PAIN

"Even if happiness forgets you a little bit, never completely forget about it." Jacques Prevert

I never changed a diaper. I don't know what to do with a baby. What do I do now? Those were my thoughts after giving birth to my son. I wondered why I didn't feel happy and tried to figure out what I needed to accomplish to make myself happy. Little did I know I was one of the millions of moms experiencing postpartum depression.

Postpartum depression occurs after childbirth. The postpartum period is within the first six weeks after giving birth, but postpartum depression usually subsides within a few months unless it's untreated. Postpartum depression is different for everyone, and when mothers experience depression past the postpartum time frame, it can be challenging to spot. According to *Medical News Today*, without treatment, postpartum depression can last for a few months up to years. When postpartum showed up in my life, I wasn't aware of what it was, and it lasted much longer than I would have liked.

Side A

As I was preparing to leave school in ninth grade, this boy barged through the door leading to the back staircase that I used to take to leave school. He caught my attention as he spoke loudly in *Patois (native Jamaican language)*. Although I didn't know him and he wasn't in my grade, I couldn't deny that he was cute. He gave me his number before leaving. Little did I know that an unexpected encounter would change everything.

His name is Andre. He was a year older than me, and we became a couple. At that age, it wasn't much to be a couple because we had so many restrictions with dating. Nonetheless, he was my boyfriend at school, and I can honestly say we were also best friends.

The relationship lasted a couple of years. When Andre became a senior in high school, he broke up with me; he told me he needed space. I was devastated. He was my first and only true love, but we remained friends after he graduated and went to college in New York.

After I graduated from high school, I went away to college, but I did not like it, so I later transferred to a school in New York. Andre was still in school in New York and while we weren't an official couple, we kept in touch. We were only friends, but I didn't pursue any other romantic relationships outside of him. Our relationship was complicated, but Andre was the love of my life. Although we had a friendly existence, it was complicated by the fact that we were too young to be seriously thinking about commitment yet neither of us wanted to see the other happily involved with anyone else. I guess it could be described as a bit toxic. He was transparent and had a way of oversharing the details of his active dating life, yet he managed to find a way to run off any of my suitors that he was aware of. Young and dumb is all I can say about this.

Party Of Three

At 19 years old, I became pregnant with Andre's child. I had so many mixed feelings about the pregnancy. I wasn't sure if Andre would support me through it. More importantly, how would I be able to graduate college and pursue a successful career with a baby? I was confused and not sure what to do. However, reality sunk in as my belly started to grow, and I began to show.

During the late nineties, women had options with what they wanted to do with their bodies. The unexpected shock of the pregnancy made me freeze instead of deciding what to do. I was also embarrassed because being pregnant early and not married was not what I was taught to do by my mother, who, of course, was very religious.

I told my mother about the pregnancy. Still unsure of what I wanted to do, but based on my mother's religious practices, I only had one option, which was to have the baby. Therefore, after I turned twenty years old, while still going to college, I became a mom to a baby boy.

The After Birth

Giving birth was a significant eye-opener. I had no idea what to do or how to be a mother. I didn't realize the magnitude of becoming a mother until after my son was born, and it was time for Andre and my mother to leave me at the hospital. After they left me alone with the baby, I was despondent. I'd had an 18 hour long and painful labor. I suffered from Anemia and lost a lot of blood during the delivery, which resulted in me going into shock after the delivery.

I thought it was over for me when I couldn't even remember my name after fainting in the bathroom after being brought to my room for my overnight stay. To say the least, I was completely and totally out of it. And there he was the cutest innocent little person who had not asked to be here. I didn't know what the heck to do with him. I could barely take care of myself. In those early hours of motherhood, I knew I was going to need courage, strength, and a whole lot of prayers! Little did I know that I was taking on the hardest yet most rewarding job that I'd ever have. Looking back now, I know it was postpartum depression. It was difficult for me to cope as a new mom.

Becoming a mother under less-than ideal circumstances left me feeling powerless because I didn't have the power to make decisions for me. With an unplanned pregnancy, I found myself questioning my self-worth and where exactly life would take me next. Trying to reconcile traditional Christian values with the fact that I was now raising a baby alone felt near impossible; it didn't fit into any storyline of success or achievement that had been previously set up by both society and how I'd grown up being taught what "normal" looked like from my family. No longer sure where I belonged in life or how - if at all - college fit anymore. Being lost became a part of my parenting journey that wasn't discussed on any new mother support sites.

Powerless to Powerful

As a new mother, I felt powerless and uncertain about my decisions. Growing up relying on my mom for answers to all of life's questions conditioned me to follow orders rather than take control. Once leaving home and into a shared space with the father of our son, who was my husband by then, something clicked inside me- it was time to trust myself enough that whatever choices I made were the right ones.

After self-reflection and counseling, I learned that I was battling postpartum depression, which is where my lack of direction and confusion came from. I didn't realize I was going through postpartum because I thought postpartum only lasted up to three months. However, I was wrong. Studies show that 38% of women with postpartum depression experience chronic symptoms and ongoing depression. (Nwadike and Brazier)

After seeking guidance and searching for answers to understand postpartum depression better, I found that various factors can create long-lasting effects if left unchecked. The mixed emotions surrounding my unplanned pregnancy had a major impact on how I felt about motherhood. Although I loved my son deeply, I was angry because it felt like someone else had decided for me before giving me time to process what having this baby would mean as it pertained to my lifestyle as a college student. While some may experience postpartum depression briefly, unfortunately, in my case, postpartum depression continued well beyond its expected duration, resulting in emotional challenges lasting several years afterward.

Side B

After analyzing my past and facing its consequences, I made a conscious effort to evolve. Unresolved anger within me blocked me from unlocking my true potential - but with professional guidance, journaling, and introspection, I was able to find inner peace again. This path eventually allowed for the healing of postpartum depression, which inevitably led to finding genuine joy in parenthood.

Remarkably through working at healing myself more deeply than ever before - an experience fulfilled by true understanding allowed me to live without apology or regret!

Today, my heart is overwhelmed with a deep-rooted love for my son - he's by far the most incredible person I've ever known. Although having him caused me to hit an unexpected roadblock on my path of joy and fulfillment, I believe it was one of the best gifts life has granted. This period of my life put me on a path to self-discovery and gave me the courage to face each day without apology. With unwavering support from my mother and husband, counseling helped provide much-needed insight into finding authentic contentment once more. Even if depression can take subtle forms that are difficult to recognize or admit aloud, happiness should always be your goal. If something stands in its way preventing you from achieving this important milestone, then don't hesitate to reach out for help.

SECTION TWO

PERSEVERING DURING TOUGH TIMES

Choose Happiness Unapologetically

TRACK 4

PERCEPTION

"The reality of life is that your perceptions — right or wrong — influence everything else you do. When you get a proper perspective of your perceptions, you may be surprised how many other things fall into place." Roger Birkman

W ho are you calling *baby momma*? A baby momma is a derogatory term used in impoverished neighborhoods and uneducated households. A baby momma isn't a college student from a Christian family. Or is she?

Our perception is a mental image of ourselves. It's how we define good qualities and challenges. Our environment, our experiences, and beliefs shape these perceptions. When perceiving oneself, our self-reflection must be in a positive light for us to be happy; Perceptions are a state of mind that affects our state of being.

My Perception: Side A

It was Thanksgiving 1997, I was six months pregnant, and learning to deal with my new reality. As my boyfriend and I became more serious, I got into the habit of spending the holidays with him and his family because of my mother's Jehovah's Witness practices. Although I was raised in a Jehovah's Witness household, I still liked celebrating the holidays. Since I couldn't celebrate at home, spending the holidays at my boyfriend's house had become a thing. This holiday, in particular, was a bit different.

As soon as I shared the news of my pregnancy, a wave of doubt flooded me. During my pregnancy, insecurities crept into my head, and feeling uncertain about the future became an almost daily occurrence. But despite doubts, I drew on strength from within to keep going. Thankfully some of my friends held me up by encouraging me during this time;

unfortunately, others saw it as a chance to try and hurt or belittle me instead.

Baby Momma

Growing up in a conservative Christian household, I learned that unwed motherhood went against my beliefs. When the term "baby momma" became a common term used in my boyfriend's culture, it was more than an uncomfortable label - because of my beliefs, it felt like a personal attack. Knowing I would fall under its definition made this even worse, but no matter what life threw at me, one thing remained certain: nobody would use that word for me.

I refused to accept the label of "baby momma." I made it clear that I was *Jamie.* I made it abundantly clear that when my child arrived, I would be known as "his or her mother." Baby momma was not a term I expected or respected.

What's Wrong?

Studies show that 64% of unwed mothers are African American and unmarried motherhood can have a lasting effect on children's lives, from struggles in school to fighting an uphill battle against poverty as adults. (Emma Johnson) This often leads to a cycle where those same kids are likely to follow in their parent's footsteps and become unmarried parents themselves. However, it wasn't the potential negative consequences of being an unwed mother that bothered me; it was the title of baby momma that enraged me. The term baby momma is one that I perceived as not good. Therefore, to reconcile things in my mind, I believed I was different and shouldn't be referred to as such.

Own Your Power

Whether it was right or wrong, I would not allow myself to be defined as such. I was not afraid to vocalize my views. Well, someone couldn't accept those boundaries and decided to play with me instead of praying for me on this day. My actions at the Thanksgiving dinner were not one of my proudest moments, but it was made clear that I wouldn't be disrespected and called out my name. It was also the moment that I knew I would not be just another baby momma.

I am happy that I stood up for my beliefs. However, this situation taught me not to let society's perception define who I was. It also taught me not to give power to my negative perceptions. I shifted from meditating on the term baby momma to planning how I could be a good mother. Focusing on the proper perception of the outcome I wanted led me to make good decisions and prevent unwanted consequences for myself and my child.

Today, my then-boyfriend and I are married, and my son is now getting a master's degree. Therefore, beating the odds against children born out of wedlock. Instead of giving into my perception of what a baby momma was, I fought to get the desired results that I wanted, which were education, marriage, and success like my mom, and I always planned. However, it wasn't in that order.

My Perception: Side A

Life isn't a series of events that happen to you; they're growth opportunities. When an obstacle appears, don't let it discourage and defeat you - use the experience as motivation. Believe in yourself, maintain realistic expectations with proper perception, and trust your ability to create positive outcomes no matter what society thinks. Life gives us plenty of chances to thrive – let those moments shape your story. What in your life do you need to switch your perception from an image of failure to your desired outcome?

Choose Happiness Unapologetically

TRACK 5

UNCOMFORTABLE

"The comfort zone is the great enemy of courage and confidence." Brian Tracy

What would you do if presented with an opportunity to achieve your biggest goal? Would you stand up and go for it? Or would you be afraid to do something new?

The definition of greatness is to stand out and be distinguished, which means the quality of being great. To achieve excellence is not going to be doing something that you know how to do or something you have done. Your highest level of greatness is when you achieve the biggest goal you did not think was within reach. Achieving that goal will require you to stretch to necessary heights in order to receive the distinction that results from it. The greatness we want in life is not gained by doing something ordinary. Therefore, we must prepare ourselves to get out of our comfort zones.

Side A

I believe that many of us are afraid of our potential. We are fearful of change and scared of achieving the level of success that we can. For many of us, this leads to procrastination. I have been guilty of this. Many researchers believe that procrastination is a coping strategy for avoiding difficult feelings such as guilt, anxiety, and self-doubt. That said, I ask you whether YOU are keeping yourself from greatness. Are there things you have yet to do and accomplishments that you'd like to check off your list? Are you putting off the challenging tasks that will enable you to achieve greatness in the future? According to Better Health, "procrastination can take mental energy, and I believe it can be draining when we do not have the proper mindset. I can relate to this very well."

I usually lead from the back or where I cannot be seen. From public speaking to writing this book, it is scary for me to reveal who I am, so writing this is a big deal. Writing is me stepping outside my comfort zone to pursue greatness.

What's the big deal, you may ask? The answer is that I like being in the background because it's comfortable there with no one to see or judge me. Regarding the speaking engagements I was booked for, I had to get increasingly uncomfortable until it became comfortable.

Side B

I'll share my story of being behind the podium. I love giving speeches, talks, and lectures. But I love doing them behind the stage. Although I know the audience can hear me from wherever I stand, the podium gives me a sense of security. I feel safe back there. In the front, I am exposed. I'm wide open and no longer in my comfort zone. However, whenever I do it while uncomfortable, I become more confident. After continuously stepping out of my comfort zone, I now have the confidence to speak in front of an audience. I run toward the opportunities to be in front of many people while performing my D.J. duty.

When my son was younger, I attended a college seminar with him and there was an excellent speaker, Derrius Quarles, author of *Million Dollar Scholar: Winning The Scholarship Race,* that helped me come to my conclusion about growing from stepping in the front. His presentation was geared toward high school students, but I was empowered and extremely inspired. He told the students that they needed to learn the strategy of being in what he identified as the "scholarship state of mind." The scholarship state of mind includes confidence, optimism, focus, and preparedness.

I challenge you to make a short list of things that are on your to-do list. Prioritize them in order of importance. Then evaluate your situation, make the necessary changes to get into the scholarship state of mind, and prepare yourself to win. I will leave you with a few of the personal mantras I adopted after listening to him:

1. Decide, commit, succeed
2. Work hard, stay humble
3. Great things come to those who work
4. The only time you should look back is to see how far you've come.

Great things never come from comfort zones. When you decide to be happy in life, it's imperative to know it requires change and bending and stretching in order to achieve the impossible. We experience the most growth leading to achieving the greatness we all have inside when we step outside from where we are comfortable.

TRACK 6

KEEP DOING IT

"Courage starts with showing up and letting ourselves be seen." Brené Brown

Let's rewind to 1977; I was standing in my crib when the Sanford and Son theme music came on. When the bass hit, I started to dance. Fast forward to 1983, my favorite R&B band of all time, New Edition, hit the scene with their single *Candy Girl*. I was at one of our many family events when I heard the song for the first time. I remember being so excited about the music.

My mom purchased my first turntable, A.K.A. "Fisher Price record player," and my first two records this same year.

One, of course, was *Candy Girl* by New Edition, and the other was Run D.M.C. The A-side was *It's like that,* and the B-side *Sucker M.C.s.* At that point, I was in music HEAVEN. At six years old, I became responsible for the music selections at our family events. Me, my Fisher Price record player, and my vinyl. I was ready to, as today's generation likes to say, "turn up."

As you can see, I've always genuinely loved music. If you ask any member of my family, then they will all tell you that I'm known as the family "hype" woman. Yes, the Fisher Price record player, my mom, New Edition, and Run D.M.C. are responsible for the birth of what is now known as the brand *Ms. Chu the D.J.*

Side A

I began pursuing my passion for DJing when I enrolled in my first class in 2006 at the Scratch D.J. Academy. I was a bedroom D.J. for several years, completely afraid of standing in front of an audience and allowing people to hear my sound. My husband is my first D.J. mentor.

My first time on the set was in front of an audience because he had to use the bathroom. I remember him asking, *"J, can you play the next two songs while I run to the bathroom?"* I looked at him like he had three heads. Here we were at an event with a room full of teenagers, a formal senior dance, and he wanted me to play the music. WHAT! I said, *"I don't even know what to do."* He gave me a crash course on loading a song, the crossfader on the mixer, and searching the computer library. Then I figured that it couldn't be too hard. I told him to go ahead and go to the bathroom.

I looked at the audience and at the two songs he told me to play next. I was not too fond of my husband's selection, so I selected my pieces. Unsure of the outcome, I played what I felt was best. Suddenly, there was a mad dash to the dance floor, and when my husband returned from the bathroom to take over, he gave me a high five and said, *"I don't know what you did, but you should keep doing it!"*

Side B

Taking the plunge into my first DJing experience was empowering - it showed me that I could be brave and go after what I wanted, no matter how scary or unexpected. Despite being inexperienced and fearing messing up in front of everyone, I was determined to show who I was. All those listening, loved the energy I brought - a unique vibe through music cultivated from daring creativity rather than conformity.

41

Believing in myself fueled my passion for DJing. Since then, I've completed several D.J. courses, trained with, and been mentored by, some of the best award-winning D.J.s in the business. Plus, I've executed 1000+ corporate and private events. My corporate client list runs the gamut from Soul Cycle to the US Open.

After facing years of depression following getting pregnant while in college, I broke free and became a passionate D.J. My first experience taught me an invaluable lesson - put yourself first if you want your joy to have its most significant impact. As I've come out on top from a tough time in my life as a pregnant college student, it's clear now more than ever. When we choose our jubilant way of being over relying solely on pleasing others, there's no limit to the kind of uplifting energy we can spread around us.

SECTION THREE

HOW TO CHOOSE HAPPINESS UNAPOLOGETICALLY

TRACK 7

HAPPY

"Happiness is when what you think, what you say, and what you do are in harmony." Mahatma Gandhi

H appy people can be annoying. You know the happy people who stop you wherever you are to wave, talk, and greet you with the biggest smile. However, we can learn from those kinds of people; Happy people are typically confident people. They believe in themselves and their ability to achieve their goals and are unafraid to be seen and heard. They don't doubt themselves or second-guess their decisions.

45

Happy people are also resilient. They know that setbacks and challenges are a part of life, but they don't let them get them down. They pick themselves up and keep going, no matter what. And finally, happy people are persistent. They don't give up easily. They keep moving forward until they reach their goals.

I've learned in both my personal life as a wife and mom and professional life in corporate America and from DJing, that if you want to be happy, then you must believe in yourself and your abilities. To believe in yourself, it's imperative to remove any unforgiveness holding you back, learn to love who you are today, and forget your past mistakes so that your strengths will be seen by you and others.

Believe In Yourself

To be confident, you must believe in yourself. It is essential to believe in oneself to be happy and successful. When you have confidence in your abilities, it allows you to persevere through difficult times and maintain a positive outlook. It also allows you to take risks and seize the opportunities that come your way.

Without belief in oneself, self-doubt, and negative thinking make it easy to become bogged down. This can lead to a spiral of negative emotions, which can be hard to break out of. On the other hand, when you believe in yourself, you are more likely to see challenges as something to overcome rather than something that will defeat you.

There are many ways to develop belief in oneself. One must consider past accomplishments and recognize how far you have come. Another is identifying and focusing on using your strengths to achieve your goals. Finally, it is important to surround yourself with supportive people who will believe in you even when you might not believe in you.

Resilience and Persistence

What does it mean to be resilient? It means being able to bounce back from setbacks and challenges. It means having the strength to keep going even when things are tough. And it means being able to adapt and change as needed. Being resilient doesn't mean that you're never going to face challenges or have any setbacks. It means that you'll be able to handle whatever comes your way and become stronger.

Persistence is another important quality for achieving happiness. You must be willing to work hard and keep going even when things get tough. When things get challenging, it's easy to give up and quit. But if you're persistent, you'll find a way through the challenges and come out victorious on the other side.

Side A

Unforgiveness

We all make mistakes, which sometimes can have dire consequences. It took me a long time to forgive myself for not having a career before having a child and for not being more prepared for the changes that came with motherhood. Until I forgave myself, I couldn't enjoy my life and accomplishments. If you are similar to me and you're struggling to forgive yourself for something you did, then it can be helpful to remember that everyone faces challenges, but we all have the capacity for growth and change. What's important is what you do after difficult situations. Do you learn from them and become a better person, or do you dwell on them and let them drag you down?

If you're having trouble forgiving yourself, then try thinking about how you would forgive someone else in the same situation. Would you be as hard on them as you are on you? Probably not. Try to cut yourself some slack and give yourself the same compassion and understanding you would extend to others.

Remember that forgiveness is a process, not a destination. It might take some time to forgive yourself fully, but keep working at it, and eventually, the weight of your past obstacles will lift.

Past Pain

Leaving the past behind is not always easy. However, it is important to remember that dwelling on the past will only prevent you from moving forward and enjoying your present. Instead of dwelling on what has already happened, focus on the present moment and what you can do to make the most of it.

The past can be a source of pain, disappointment, and regret. It can be difficult to move on when we are stuck in the same behavior patterns and thinking that lead us down a destructive path. But we must remember that the past does not define our future. We can choose to make different choices and live in the present with an attitude of hope and possibility.

It is important to recognize that we can choose how to respond to our experiences. We can choose to forgive ourselves for mistakes we have made and learn from them so that we do not repeat them in the future. We can also see our mistakes as valuable lessons that help us grow as individuals. Letting go of the past will enable us to move forward.

It is not always easy to leave the past behind, but it is possible. The key is to focus on the present moment and take actionable steps to make positive changes in your life. Allow yourself to experience the full range of emotions related to the past, accept them without judgment, and then make a conscious decision to let go and move forward. Commit yourself to take one small step each day towards creating a better future for you. With this approach, you can create a life of joy, contentment, and happiness.

Side B

Leadership

I was letting my past mistakes hold me back. I had the "Always the assistant, I'd rather not be the boss" mentality. I participated in a training where I did an exercise that helped me understand how I show up in the world. I was viewed as a leader by my peers and had leadership qualities but was not comfortable making the hard decisions. I'd rather help the boss get the win by advising and doing a great job as support but did not want to bear the responsibility of things going wrong.

I learned that because of the way I'd perceived myself after having my son at 20 years old, I questioned all of my decisions going forward. I was always scared to make what I'd consider, "the wrong move," when I had made all the right moves even though I was still second guessing myself after having a baby.

At that moment, I learned to celebrate my accomplishments, understand I wasn't a statistic, and I was educated. I was the top ranked female executive at my firm, and yet I was still trying to hide behind the young lady who was fearful and not sure of herself because she had a baby before marriage. This training literally changed my life.

Forgiving myself for past decisions was an important step to move on from the past. Letting go of my anger and resentment towards myself allowed me to move forward with a positive outlook. Uncovering that my past was holding me back was crucial to my current success. Use your experiences as opportunities to grow and become a better person. Remember that every day is a new opportunity to start fresh and be happy.

Self-Love

Self-love is one of the most important things you can give yourself to forgive yourself and leave the past behind you. It's the foundation for a happy and fulfilling life. You will be more happy, resilient, and persistent when you love yourself. You're also more likely to attract positive people and experiences into your life. Self-love doesn't mean being selfish or self-centered. It means having a healthy regard for yourself and taking care of yourself emotionally and physically, enabling you to put past mistakes behind you and forgive.

Self-love is also setting boundaries, saying "no" when needed, and doing what's best for you even if it's not what others want or expect from you. Developing self-love takes time and practice, but it's worth it. A strong foundation of self-love can help you to weather any storm that comes your way with grace.

How-To Walk-In Self-Love

It is so easy today to get caught up in what everyone else is doing and compare ourselves to others. We are constantly bombarded with images of "perfect" lives and bodies, and it can be hard to love ourselves when we don't measure up. But the truth is, comparison is the thief of joy, and you deserve to be happy, unapologetically! Here are some tips on how-to walk-in self-love so you can live a happier life:

1. Forgive yourself: We all make mistakes and forgiving yourself for them is important. Holding onto anger and resentment will only drag you down.

2. Be kind: Talk to yourself like you would talk to a friend. Be encouraging and understanding.

3. Take care of yourself: Physical self-care is important, but so is emotional and mental self-care.

Ensure you get enough sleep, eat healthy foods, exercise, and do things you enjoy.

4. Set boundaries: Say no when you need to, and don't be afraid to put yourself first. You deserve love and respect.

5. Surround yourself with positive people: Spend time with people who make you feel good about yourself and support your self-love journey.

What does happiness mean to you? To me it means that no matter what life throws my way - good or bad - I can remain positive and focus on the good. It means taking responsibility for my happiness and not allowing anyone or anything to control how I feel about myself and my life. And it means never giving up, even when things are tough or don't go as planned. Ultimately, happiness begins and ends with me learning to love myself and doing what's right for me. Therefore, love yourself, believe in yourself, and forget past disappointments to pursue your true happy place.

TRACK 8

THE CHOICE IS YOURS

"Life is all about making choices. Always do your best to make the right ones, and always do your best to learn from the wrong ones." Asad Meah

When you look at your life, what do you see? Do you see happiness and contentment, or do you see struggle and hardship? Like most people, you probably see a mixture of both. The way we view our life and choices dictate our outcomes. After I had an unplanned pregnancy, I focused on that which kept me feeling down. No matter what I accomplished, it was difficult for me to celebrate my wins because I was too busy being hard on myself for my past decisions. The crucial part about being happy is that our happiness is shaped by our views on who we are, what we want, what we've done, and what we have.

We decide how we view things. The choice to focus on good things and be happy is up to us. The first step to choosing happiness unapologetically, as discussed in the previous chapter, is to have confidence and belief in ourselves despite our past disappointments. The next step is to recognize happiness is a choice and to choose it.

There's no question that happiness is a choice. And, like any choice, it isn't always easy. But here's why you should choose happiness: When you're happy, you're more likely to be productive. Happiness increases motivation and energy, making you more likely to get things done. Happy people are also more likely to be successful. Studies have shown that happy people are more likely to achieve their goals and be successful in their careers.

Whatever happiness means to you, realize that you can choose it. No one else can choose it for you. And don't apologize for choosing happiness! If you want to be happy, then start by deciding to be happy. Take action steps each day to move closer to your goal. Be resilient when setbacks happen and persist even when things get tough.

Side A

Trust Your Choices

For so long, I listened to the voice of others and did what was expected of me without considering what I wanted. When we allow the voice of others to dictate how we feel, we are giving away our power. We are silencing our inner voice and choosing to live according to someone else's standards. It is not a recipe for happiness. Making decisions based on what feels good can be difficult when we are constantly bombarded with messages telling us to do the opposite. Society tells us that we should be focused on success and achievement and that happiness is a secondary goal. However, research has repeatedly shown that happy people are more likely to succeed personally and professionally.

To be happy, you must learn to trust yourself and your choices. Too often, we second-guess ourselves and allow others to dictate what makes us happy. We need to remember that we are in charge of our happiness. It can be difficult to trust yourself, especially if you regret past decisions like I did.

But it's important to remember that everyone makes mistakes. Mistakes aren't a loss if you learn from them and move forward; Mistakes are a lesson that enables you to produce future good experiences after learning from prior ones.

Happiness is also contagious. Those around you are also more likely to be happy when you're happy. By choosing happiness, you're making yourself more satisfied and those around you more comfortable. Finally, happy people live longer and healthier lives. Studies have shown that happiness leads to improved physical health and longevity. Not only will choosing happiness improve your life in the short term, but it will also improve your long-term health.

New Way Of Thinking

The idea of choosing happiness is nothing new. We've heard the phrase "choose happiness" many times, but what does it mean? It means changing how we think and behave, breaking away from the traditional thinking of letting life dictate our happiness, and instead making conscious choices to be happy. It means being resilient and persistent despite adversity rather than succumbing to sadness or depression. It means actively working towards being happy every day, no matter how difficult or challenging life may seem. Choosing happiness unapologetically requires a different mindset that believes in the power of choice and actively works towards creating a happier life for oneself.

Instead of expecting things to happen independently, choosing happiness encourages us to take responsibility for our emotions and behaviors and make decisions that will benefit us in the long run. For me, this involved learning healthier coping skills such as mindfulness meditation, participating in meaningful activities like volunteering, and engaging in positive self-talk instead of negative self-talk.

Resilience and persistence are also important components of choosing happiness. Having resilience when faced with obstacles helps us remain positive even in tough situations, while persistence can help us stay motivated when things get tough. Ultimately, when we choose happiness, we are more likely to create a better quality of life for ourselves and those around us.

If you're anything like me, then you've been through some tough times. You've been heart broken, repeatedly disappointed, and faced challenges and setbacks. It's easy to become jaded and lose hope that things will improve. But I'm here to tell you that they can, and they will.

It all starts with a change in mindset. Instead of wallowing in self-pity and feeling sorry for yourself, choose happiness, and refuse to let the negative thoughts take over. When you decide to be happy, your whole life changes. You'll find yourself attracted to different things, people, and situations. Everything will start falling into place, and you'll be amazed at how good life can be. Don't wait to choose happiness.

Side B:

Visualize Your Success

Regarding happiness, our brains are wired to focus on the negative. This is known as the negativity bias, and it's something that we all have to work against. To be truly happy, requires us to consciously focus on the positive and forget about the negative things that happened in the past.

One way to do this is through visualization. When you take the time to visualize what you want, you're more likely to achieve it. Whether visualizing your ideal life or picturing yourself having a great day, focusing on what makes you happy can make a big difference.

Follow Your Gut

When making decisions, listening to your heart and intuition is important. These inner guides will always steer you in the right direction, even if sometimes it doesn't make sense logically. Trusting your gut feelings may not always be easy, but it is vital if you want to lead a happy and fulfilling life.

Of course, there will be times when making decisions based on what feels good does not work out perfectly. Life is full of ups and downs, and there is no guarantee that everything will always go our way. However, following our intuition increases our chances of living a life we love.

Choose To Be Happy

Ready to choose happiness? Here are some things I did on my journey to happiness; It worked for me, and I hope it works for you:

1. Acknowledge your feelings and permit yourself to feel them. Don't question if your feelings are right or wrong. Embrace them and self-reflect to make the best choices based on your desires.
2. Reframe your negative thoughts and focus on the positive. It took me a while to do this, but once I

could change my thoughts, I could enjoy my family and my life.

3. Practice gratitude and celebrate even small victories. Many of us struggle to see the beauty in things, be grateful for what we have, and find hope in tough times, but this is necessary for our quest to choose a happy life.

4. Don't take things personally. Life is full of ups and downs, but it's important to remember that none are about YOU. What other people say or do is their business, not yours. Don't take it personally when someone cuts you off in traffic or yells at you at work. Let it roll off your back and move on with your day.

5. Don't compare yourself to others. It is a recipe for disaster. There will always be someone who has more than or less than you. Comparisons are useless and only serve to make you feel bad.

It's important to remember happiness is a choice. It's not something that happens to us; it's something we must pursue actively. Achieving happiness takes trusting our choices and learning to follow our gut. Things may not always go as planned, but that's where resilience and persistence comes in. Choose to be happy today by any means necessary. The choice is yours.

TRACK 9

GET UP, STAND UP

"Finding your voice is about having the confidence to know you matter so you can use your voice." Jen Mueller

Are you afraid of taking risks or of not being accepted if you go against the grain? Do you feel overwhelmed by the expectations of those around you? Or maybe you feel pressure to conform to what is expected of you. Standing out from the crowd and choosing a different path can be difficult. As a result, it can be hard to discover who you are and what makes you unique.

When choosing happiness, the first step is believing in yourself and having confidence, followed by recognizing that you have a choice to be happy. The next step in your happiness journey is to find your voice and use it unapologetically.

Finding Your Voice

Finding your voice can mean many things, but at its core, it is about owning who you are and what you believe in. It means standing up for your beliefs and living on your terms.

To find your voice is to recognize and honor your true feelings, thoughts, and values while you strive to do and achieve your best. It takes courage to follow your dreams and pursue what makes you happy without apologizing. However, when you find your voice, it empowers you to make decisions leading to greater joy and fulfillment.

In search of your voice, you may be fighting an internal battle between doing what society tells you to do versus following your heart and intuition. Don't be afraid to challenge traditional beliefs and ideologies if they don't align with what is true for you. Make room for creative expression and curiosity, allowing yourself to explore new ideas and perspectives that may take you out of your comfort zone. Finding your voice requires resilience and persistence, as it often involves pushing back against cultural norms or standards that don't feel right to you. Nonetheless, communicate authentically and with conviction so that your opinion is heard and respected.

Unapologetic

Unapologetic means acting without making excuses and living life in a manner that is true to oneself without having to make excuses for it. It is about being strong enough to accept and embrace yourself without apology, and being unapologetic means owning your decisions, actions, life, and being proud of yourself. It is about having the courage to stand up for yourself, despite any judgment or criticism from others. When you choose happiness unapologetically, trust that your voice will help you create your desired future if you keep pushing forward.

Side A

Why it's Hard

It can be hard to identify your voice. You may have conflicting feelings or ideas about what you want to say. Your inner voice may be drowned out by external messages that tell you how to think, act, and feel. All these things can make it challenging to identify your true self and let your authentic voice shine through.

Take note of when fear or self-doubt creeps in and uses these moments as opportunities to practice self-compassion and kindness. Always remember that, ultimately, you can choose how you respond to any situation and how you want to live your life.

How to Find your Voice

How

How do you find your voice? It starts with getting to know yourself on a deeper level. What are your values? What are your passions? What makes you feel alive? Once you understand who you are better, it will be easier to start expressing yourself in a way that is true to YOU.

Being honest and transparent about who you are and what matters most can be influential in finding your voice. When you embrace the person you are, you will feel more confident in your decisions and the direction you want to go in life.

Finding your voice is a personal journey, of understanding your values and beliefs and what makes you feel fulfilled. No one else knows how to find your voice except you because you are the only person who knows what brings you joy and fulfillment. Permit yourself to be yourself without apology. This process of self-discovery is not always easy, but it is critical so you can choose happiness.

It's easy to get swept up in a cycle of negative thinking and feeling overwhelmed by our circumstances, but we can choose to act and do something different. Taking the time to understand your thoughts and feelings can be incredibly valuable in this process.

Side B

Sounds of Joy

As a DJ, finding your voice is finding your unique sound, playing music unapologetically, and being confident the crowd will cheer for you with excitement. This was a scary thing for me to do.

As I mentioned earlier in the book, when I was DJing with my husband, and I had to fill in for him while he went to the bathroom, I was in a quandary. *Should I play songs he hand-picked or find my selection?* When I followed my gut and played what I wanted, not only was I identifying my sound, but I also helped the crowd have more fun. That was the beginning of me identifying my unique DJ style.

Since then, I've executed thousands of corporate and private events. My corporate client list runs the gamut from Soul Cycle to Tesla. I've spun store grand openings, professional sports games, charitable events, and Simon Properties events and concerts. This would not have been possible without me finding my voice, my unique sound.

Own It

When taking ownership of your happiness, it's imperative to find your voice and use it confidently and unapologetically. Putting yourself out there and speaking up can be difficult, especially if you've been conditioned to be quiet. But having a strong voice is essential to creating and maintaining happiness.

Don't be afraid to be yourself; trust your choices. Never forget that you have the right to be heard. There is nothing wrong with speaking up and using your voice, so do it unapologetically and without fear. Once you become comfortable expressing your thoughts, feelings, and beliefs, you will find it easier to find joy and happiness.

Here are some tips to find and use your voice:

1. **Be yourself.** It is the most important thing. Don't try to be someone you're not. Be authentic to yourself, and your voice will shine through.

2. **Doing what you love:** Doing what you love could be your job, hobby, or creative outlet. If you love your work and attitude, then it will show in your career.

3. **Being around people, you love** Spending time with loved ones is a surefire way to boost your happiness. Whether it's family, friends, or pets, being around those you care about will make you feel good.

4. **Having a positive outlook:** Happiness is a state of mind. Focusing on the positive things in life makes you more likely to be happy. Similarly, if you let go of negative thoughts and emotions, you'll open yourself up to happiness.

5. **Laughing:** Laughter is one of the quickest ways to feel happier. It's also contagious, so those around you will likely join in if you start laughing.

6. **Getting outside:** Fresh air and nature have improved moods and mental health. Get out there and enjoy the great outdoors.

7. **Stand up for what you believe in.** You'll find your voice more easily when you stand up for what you believe in. Have conviction and be passionate about what you're saying.

8. **Be resilient.** Don't give up if something doesn't work out how you initially wanted it to.

9. **Be persistent.** Keep going even if others don't agree with you and agree to disagree.

10. **Believe in yourself.** Your voice matters the most to you. If you don't believe in yourself, no one else will either. Have faith in yourself and your abilities and speak up with everything you've got.

Being true to yourself and embracing your voice gives you the strength to take risks and pursue your goals. It encourages you to live authentically, embrace your uniqueness, and not try to be anyone else.

Having a clear understanding of yourself and how you want to live will also give you clarity in making tough decisions. Let your future goals guide you as you consider the options before you so that you can stay focused and intentional as you strive for your vision of success. Remember, there is no room for self-doubt or second-guessing when speaking your truth. Stand up and be brave. Show the world who you are and what is right for you.

TRACK 10

SHUT 'EM DOWN

"When someone shows you who they are,
believe them the first time." Maya Angelou-

What do you do when no one is looking? Are you still a kind person with a loving heart, or do you treat people unworthily if no one is around to hold you accountable?

The final step in choosing happiness unapologetically is to separate to elevate and reach your full potential. To do this, it is essential to know which character traits are acceptable by others versus those you will not tolerate. When you separate to elevate, you perform the self-care needed for your well-being. It is not selfish to do self-care; it is necessary to choose happiness unapologetically.

Integrity

Who are you spending time with? Are they encouraging you to speak up and go after your dreams, or are they discouraging you and keeping you low? Managing your life is your core responsibility, so handle it well.

How do you define a person with integrity? I think of a person with integrity as someone who loves and respects themselves and others, makes wise choices, is selfless, and does things in decency and order. People prove their integrity over time, so you learn to trust them to constantly act with a sense of integrity. Although everyone has a rough day, if someone consistently shows you the contrary of what you prefer, then you are required to protect your peace, your environment, and separate from them.

Toxicity

A toxic person adds upset and stress to your life, which is usually due to their lack of happiness or other issues they have. Toxic people may be good at times, but their true character eventually manifests, so pay attention to the signs they display.

It's important to examine all of the people in your life to determine if they are adding to your happiness or preventing it.

To choose happiness unapologetically, we must choose the people we let into our lives and how long they stay in it. It doesn't matter if it's family members or other people we love for past things they've done to us. What have they consistently done lately? This is a question you should be asking yourself.

I've learned that just because you've known a person for a long time and maybe even grew up with them, when you notice indecent behaviors that are repetitive, you cannot ignore their deviant behavior because of your love and loyalty. Just because you've known someone for a long time, it does not give them the ability to add chaos to your life.

Side A

In December 2016, I was on the beautiful island of Jamaica, one of my favorite places in the world. At the time, I was physically and emotionally drained. I knew I shouldn't have gone on the trip. Instead of bowing out of the trip gracefully because I was dealing with a serious family issue and lacked mental capacity, I chose to celebrate my friend's graduation.

While in Jamaica, I was asked to provide my DJ services, and I was ecstatic because this would be my first international experience. This opportunity felt invigorating, not only because it was my goal to be an international DJ but also because I was dealing with an intense family issue and needed good news.

When my friend found out about the DJing opportunity, the friend I came to support, who knew I was dealing with turmoil and barely holding on, became upset. She did not want me to entertain anything else in Jamaica that did not involve her graduation celebrations. Even though the DJ opportunity did not clash with any of the events she had planned, she was distraught and created a pretty tense environment for me. Later on, I learned that she didn't want me to Dj while on her birthday trip, (even though it was after her graduation) because she felt as though I was making the trip about me, where she felt as though everything should be about her.

This was an awful experience because I was already mentally drained, but I found joy in the opportunity to DJ in Jamaica. My friend added further stress when she became outraged because I had a DJing gig. This made me regret going to Jamaica because my gut said to stay home. Yet, I thought I was putting my integrity first because I had agreed to go on the trip before the personal stress settled into my life

By going to Jamaica, I put my friend first. However, when I chose to do something for myself, my friend wanted me to put her feelings first again. If I'm always putting my friend first and my friend also puts herself first, then who is taking care of me? Consequently, after one horrible encounter in Jamaica followed by another, I realized that choosing happiness unapologetically is not supporting people above taking care of myself and enjoying my life. This trip emphasized that self-care should be pursued above everything else.

Side B

Self-Care

When you are stressed, you are less able to unwind and slowdown, which makes you feel more anxious and overwhelmed by even the simplest tasks; this is an indication that you need to prioritize your self-care. Self-care means taking care of yourself and everything that pertains to enhancing your life. If you do not practice self-care, then you will not be able to be well, do your job, or care for others. Self-care is the answer for you to do everything you need and want to accomplish daily.

The physical, mental, and emotional benefits of self-care increases your health and well-being. Research suggests that self-care promotes positive health outcomes, such as fostering resilience, living longer, and better managing stress.

Self-care requires checking in and asking yourself how you're doing and what your body's asking for. Some people use it to deal with complex news stories, while others to maintain happiness. Self-care does not mean the same thing for everyone. Different people will adopt different self-care practices, and your self-care needs will change over time. However, choosing the right people to hang around, those with integrity, will always be a form of self-care.

How do you know when it's time to separate from toxic people?

After a draining interaction with them, it quickly becomes clear that they have mastered the art of manipulation. Whether it's intimidation tactics to get their own way or guilt-tripping you for control, toxic people will stoop low in order to secure what they want. Furthermore, jealousy and defensiveness come to the surface at even the smallest reminder of competition - and don't forget those condescending backhanded compliments.

Here are eight signs that you need to separate because you are dealing with a toxic person.

1. You're left feeling emotionally exhausted after an encounter with them.
2. They try to intimidate you to get their way.
3. They try to control you by guilt tripping.
4. They are easily jealous.
5. They constantly see themselves as a victim.
6. They give backhanded compliments
7. They are overly defensive.
8. They are unwilling to support you.

Today, I no longer focused on that awful experience I had in Jamaica or my now former friend. What I choose to focus on is the lesson learned from the series of unpleasant events.

Above all else, after that experience I realized that it is completely impossible to pour from an empty cup. When you are depleted, you cannot be of service to anyone. Take whatever time you need to heal yourself and do it unapologetically. The people who are meant to be in your life, who love you and want to see you at your best will understand. They will also greet you with open arms once you have healed.

Choose Happiness Unapologetically

Although my former friend tried to manipulate me to cater to her, I chose happiness unapologetically and I took the DJ gig. I chose to separate to elevate and now I am an international DJ! I tore the place down with my positive and upbeat energy.

When I arrived at the DJ booth in Jamaica, everyone was looking at me including the other DJ wondering who's this chick? Two songs later, the entire club was bouncing! They enjoyed my confidence, felt the happiness I decided to embrace, and they loved my unique sound. I shut the place down! (mic drop)

To choose happiness unapologetically means to choose YOU! This will require you to leave some people behind and not show up for others who don't support you. Let me offer you a gentle reminder that people come into your life for a reason, a season or a lifetime. And once their season is up, it's OK to let them go.

CONCLUSION

Choosing happiness unapologetically means having the courage and strength to love ourselves and make the most of our lives, even when times get tough. It's about recognizing what happiness looks like for you and going after it without fear of judgment or failure.

Begin each day by mentioning something - no matter how small - you appreciate about yourself, as this will remind you that you are enough.

Find your voice, and never settle for anything less than your best. Embrace every challenge and obstacle as an opportunity to grow and evolve. Rely on your inner strength to fuel your drive and propel you forward.

Choosing life's happiness comes from within and is not dependent on others. This process may require us to step back from people or situations not aligned with our higher vision for ourselves. Staying true to who we are can often come with resistance. However, it is necessary if we strive to elevate, set goals, and grow in pursuit of becoming our best selves.

Above all, remember that choosing happiness doesn't mean ignoring difficulties. Instead, it's about rising above them with resilience and persistence.

WORKS CITED

"Brian Tracy Quote." AzQuotes, 2023,
     https://www.azquotes.com/quote/1069380.

"Courage Starts with Showing up and Letting Ourselves Be
     Seen. -Brené Brown." Blue Lilac Marketing, 15 Oct.
     2019,
     https://www.bluelilacmarketing.com/amp/2019/10/
     15/courage-starts-with-showing-up-and-letting-
     ourselves-be-seen-bren%C3%A9-brown.

"Jacques Prevert Quotes." BrainyQuote, Xplore,
     https://www.brainyquote.com/quotes/jacques_preve
     rt_144552.

"Jocko Willink Quotes." BrainyQuote, Xplore,
     https://www.brainyquote.com/quotes/jocko_willink
     _8644.

Johnson, Emma. "Single Mother Statistics for 2023:
     Surprising Facts about Single Moms."
     Wealthysinglemommy.com, 1 Mar. 2023,
     https://www.wealthysinglemommy.com/single-
     mom-statistics/.

"Mahatma Gandhi Quotes." BrainyQuote, 2023,
https://www.brainyquote.com/quotes/mahatma_gan
dhi_105593.

Meah, Asad. "34 Inspirational Quotes on Choices."
AwakenTheGreatnessWithin, May 2023,
https://www.awakenthegreatnesswithin.com/34-
inspirational-quotes-choices/.

Mueller, Jen. "5 Quotes to Inspire You to Find Your Voice."
Talk Sporty to Me, 21 Oct. 2020,
https://www.talksportytome.com/blog/5-quotes-to-
inspire-you-to-find-your-voice.

Nwadike, Valinda Riggins, and Yvette Brazier. "Postpartum
Depression: How Long Does It Last?" Medical News
Today, 5 Nov. 2019,
https://www.medicalnewstoday.com/articles/271217
#risk-factors.

Ralliford, Jamie. Choose Happiness Unapologetically With
Resilience And Persistence. 2023.

"Reasons Why People Procrastinate: Do You Need to
Change Your Habits?" BetterHelp, 26 Apr. 2033,
https://www.betterhelp.com/advice/procrastination/
18-symptoms-and-causes-of-chronic-procrastination/.

Smith, Sylvia. ``15 Ways Cognitive Behavioral Therapy
Benefits Couples." Marriage Advice, 27 Sept. 2022,
https://www.marriage.com/advice/therapy/cognitive
-behavioral-therapy-helps-relationship/.

"Tips on Effective Coaching with Birkman." Birkman,
https://blog.birkman.com/tips-on-effective-
coaching-with-
birkman#:~:text=Roger%20Birkman%2C%20the%2
0creator%20of,other%20things%20fall%20into%20pl
ace.

"Transform Your Life: Understanding The Signs of Low
Self-Esteem." BetterHelp, 25 Apr. 2023,
https://www.betterhelp.com/advice/self-
esteem/signs-of-low-self-esteem-and-what-to-do-
about-it/.

ABOUT THE AUTHOR

Jamie S. Ralliford, affectionately known as "Ms. Chu," is a mother, wife, corporate executive, entrepreneur, international DJ, influencer, and transformational leader that is passionate about helping others maximize their full potential. Jamie is also the CEO of Bold & Boss Boutique and Bold & Boss Hair, a lifestyle brand curating style, luxury hair extensions, and custom wigs and training for the fabulous woman on the go.

A native New Yorker hailing from the borough of Queens; her edgy, city girl aura is perfectly balanced by her infectious enthusiasm for music, entrepreneurship, fashion, and serving the community at large. Jamie is the go-to person for good fun, great music, inspiration, and style. She considers herself a "chameleon" all things changing, always grooving, mover and shaker, lover of music, style, fashion and the LIFE of ANY PARTY!

She received her Bachelor of Science in Finance, Master of Business Administration in Management and Paralegal Certification from Long Island University, Brooklyn Campus.

In addition, she is also an active member of Alpha Kappa Alpha Sorority, Incorporated, Associate Member of Jack & Jill of America, Inc., and Toastmasters International.

Past clients include Tesla, Manhattan Motor Group, US Open, Macy's, Pink, and Bloomingdale's .